Guide to Small Business Insurance Coverage

A Step by Step Guide to Managing Risk In Your Business

By Meir Liraz

Published by BizMove
www.bizmove.com

Table of Contents

1. Introduction

The subjects discussed in this risk management guide should heighten your awareness of business insurance and encourage you to consider carefully the various insurance programs and options available on the market.

It is imperative that all small business owners and managers understand the various aspects of insurance and how it can help a firm be more successful.

Your Independent Agent is your key to protecting your business and ultimately, contributing to your success. Multiline agencies can provide a comprehensive range of employee benefits, property/casualty and financial services to small businesses.

In addition to helping you identify, minimize and in some instances eliminate business risks, this risk management guide includes a Checklist to help you strengthen your insurance program and provide guidelines for discussions you should have with a qualified insurance professional. A Glossary of Insurance Terms is also included to provide simple definitions for the highly technical terms you will encounter when selecting insurance for your business.

Risk Management And The Small Business

Is your business a risky business? You bet! Every small business is. Just think for a minute about the hundreds of things that most business owners worry about. A few are predictable or, at the very least, are items that you can plan for and perhaps even control to a certain extent, such as:

expected sales volume

salary costs

taxes

overhead expenses

equipment and supply costs

the price you charge for the goods or services you offer to your customers

Others are unpredictable, largely beyond your control. Examples of these unpredictable risks include:

actions your competitors may take

changing tastes and trends

the effect they have on your market and your customers

the local economy and its impact on your customer base (plant closings or unemployment, for example).

And then there are the events that can and do happen to small businesses all the time. They could directly affect your day-to-day operations, impact profits, and result in unexpected financial losses that may be serious enough to cripple your business or even bankrupt it. You've probably already considered the most obvious risks and have bought insurance to protect against the financial losses that could result from them. Most business owners recognize the loss potential from fire and injury.

Fire could damage or destroy the building your firm occupies and turn the building's contents into a pile of smoking rubbish. Whether you rent or own, your place of business and your ability to continue to do business may both be seriously affected.

If someone is injured on business premises, or injured by a product you manufacture or market, or because of the way your firm performed a service, your firm may be held responsible for that person's medical bills, lost wages or even loss of future income.

Loss of property from fire and liability for injury to another person (or another person's property) are familiar exposures. But there are hundreds of other losses and liabilities that every small business faces, many of which are often overlooked or ignored.

Large corporations often employ a full-time "risk manager" to identify and analyze possible exposures to loss or liability. The risk manager then takes steps to protect the firm against accidental and preventable loss and to minimize the financial consequences of losses that cannot be prevented or avoided. But most small businesses can't afford the services of a risk manager, even part-time, so the business owner often has to take on that responsibility.

What Is "Risk Management"?

Regardless of who does it, risk management consists of:

1. Identifying and analyzing the things that may

cause loss.

2. Choosing the best way of dealing with each of these potentials for loss.

You've worked hard to build your business, and you've poured a lot of time, effort and money into identifying loss exposures.

2. Identifying and Analyzing Exposures to Loss

Identifying exposures is a vital first step: until you know the scope of all possible losses, you won't be able to develop a realistic, cost-effective strategy for dealing with them. The last thing you want to do is come up with a superficial BandAid approach that may cause more problems than it solves.

It is not easy to recognize the hundreds of hazards, or perils that can lead to an unexpected loss. Unless you've experienced a fire, for example, you may not realize how extensive fire loss can be. Damage to the building and its contents are obvious exposures, but you should also consider:

the damage or destruction that smoke or water from dozens of fire hoses can create.

damage to employees' property (coats, tools and personal belongings) and to property belonging to others (data-processing equipment you lease or customers' property left with you for inspection or repair, for example).

the amount of business you'll lose during the weeks (or months) it takes to get back to normal again.

the loss to competitors of customers who may not

return when you reopen for business.

You begin the process of identifying exposures by taking a close look at each of your business operations and asking yourself:

1. "What could cause a loss"? If there are dozens of exposures you may find dozens of answers.

For each exposure you identify, ask yourself:

2. "How serious is that loss"? (This question helps you focus on the possible severity of each exposure. What kind of price tag, in dollars and cents, applies to that exposure?) The purpose here is not to determine where the money will come from, but how costly the loss could be.

Many business owners use a "risk analysis" questionnaire or survey as a checklist. These are available from insurance agents, most of whom will provide the expertise to help you with your analysis. With their expertise and experience, you're less likely to overlook any exposures. They'll also be available to answer your questions when you try to determine how serious a loss from a given exposure may be.

What Kinds Of Exposures Should I Look For?

In general, most questionnaires and surveys address the potential for:

property losses

business interruption losses

liability losses

key person losses

automobile losses

3. Property Losses

Property losses stem from one of the following:

physical damage to property

loss of use of property

criminal activity

Physical Damage

Property damage can be caused by many common perils: fire, windstorm, lightning and vandalism may be the first that come to mind. And it's a rare business that doesn't buy insurance to protect against these. But to cope effectively with the possibility of physical damage to property, the business owner should consider more than just damage to or destruction of the building itself.

Contents may be even more susceptible: manufacturers might lose both raw materials and finished goods that were ready to be shipped. Merchants may lose valuable inventories and fixtures. Any business might lose valuable accounting records (making it difficult to bill customers or collect from customers who owe money). Vital machinery or equipment may become inoperable because of fire and, if replacements can't be found and installed immediately, the business may even be forced into a temporary shutdown. (A detailed discussion of business interruption is provided later.)

Loss of Use

Your business could lose the use of property without suffering any physical damage. A government agency can close a manufacturer for violating health and safety regulations. The local health department may close a restaurant because of unsanitary conditions. A gas-main break or downed utility lines may shut down an entire block for one or more days.

Criminal Activity

Small businesses may also be susceptible to crimes committed by others. Burglary and robbery are obvious perils, but don't overlook possible exposure to white-color crime, employee theft, embezzlement or forgery. Merchants, in particular, may need protection against losses caused by acceptance of forged checks or unauthorized use of credit cards.

Obviously, the property exposures a bank faces are

different from those that a painting contractor, a delicatessen or a bookstore faces. An experienced insurance agent is familiar with exposures to property loss in many different kinds of business. Just as you rely on an accountant to guide you through the maze of tax regulations and record-keeping requirements, you can rely on an experienced insurance professional to help you identify the exposures to loss that your business may face.

The four kinds of exposure we've examined are only part of the story of risk and business. Another major exposure is business interruption.

4. Business interruption Losses

You have already seen how a direct loss from fire can shut down a business temporarily. Although property insurance provides money for repairing or rebuilding physical damage that is a direct result of a fire, most property policies do not cover indirect losses, such as the income that is lost while the business is interrupted for the repairs.

A special kind of insurance will cover indirect losses that occur when a direct loss (that results from a covered peril, such as fire) forces a temporary interruption of business. For example:

Weather damage to a toy store in October was repaired by late November and stocks replenished. But by then, it was too late in the Christmas selling season for the store to approach normal sales. Instead of earning the usual 55 percent of its annual volume in December, it earned only 15 percent. A 40 percent loss!

If a prep school that burns down in August can't reopen until November, the school may lose half, or even all, of a school year's tuition.

Business interruption insurance would reimburse

policyholders for the difference between normal income and the income that is earned during the enforced shutdown period.

Not only is income reduced or cut off completely during such interruptions, but also many business expenses continue such as taxes, loan payments, salaries to key employees, interest, depreciation and utilities. Without income to pay for these expenses, the business is forced to dip into reserves.

Interruption often triggers extra expenses. For example, a business may authorize overtime to shorten the interruption period, or it may reopen with a skeleton staff (additional payroll) in temporary quarters (additional rent) using leased furniture and equipment (additional overhead). These extra expenses put an additional strain on finances at a time when little if any income is being produced.

A firm can even buy business interruption insurance to protect against interruptions triggered by direct loss on someone else's property.

If a key supplier is shut down by a fire and can't deliver critical raw materials to a manufacturer, the manufacturer's business may be interrupted just as effectively as if the supplier's factory has burned to the ground.

Property damage at the key customer's business may have the same effect. If you depend upon the customer for most of your volume, and that firm's interruption causes them to suspend purchasing, you may be left holding the bag. Their interruption has caused you to lose income.

Every year hundreds of businesses that carry adequate insurance against direct loss of property fail because they overlook the possibility of indirect loss. Don't forget to protect your business against loss of income and unusual expenses that may result if direct loss forces you to close temporarily.

5. Liability Loss

Every business also faces exposures to liability loss. A business may become legally liable (i.e., responsible for payment) for bodily injury suffered by another person or persons, or for damage to or destruction of the property of others. This liability may be the result of:

A court decision (as in a lawsuit charging negligence)

Statutory provisions (such as a workers' compensation law)

Violation of contract provisions (a contract that makes one party responsible for certain kinds of losses)

Public Liability

A business may be held liable for injuries or other losses suffered by a member of the general public as the result of the firm's (or its employees') negligence or fault.

A customer in the firm's building trips on a broken step.

A defect in a product causes injury to its user.

A workman who installs a ceiling fan a customer has purchased fails to secure it properly. The fan falls, injuring the customer.

A secretarial firm rents one floor in an office building and signs a lease that holds the tenant (rather than the building owner) responsible for any third party claims for injury or property damage occurring in or on the rented space.

Your daily paper will provide dozens of other examples. A firm that is found legally liable for harming a third party will have to pay damages to compensate the injured party. In cases involving violation of a statute that protects the community as a whole, the court may also award a fine in hopes of discouraging future violations.

Regardless of who wins or looses such a suit, litigation is time-consuming and expensive. No matter how ridiculous or unfounded the suit may be, productive business hours are still lost, lawyers still have to be retained and paid and other related cost have to be met.

6. Liability to Employees

The government has enacted some sort of legislation that protects the interest of employees who are injured or who contract a disease as a result of job-related activities.

Workers' compensation laws require most employers to compensate employees for loss of income or medical expenses that are a result of work-related disease or injury (except for certain self-inflicted injuries). Should an employee die, as a result of a job-related accident or disease, the employee's family also collects a specified amount.

So far, the exposures we have looked at have all been more or less external to the business. There are, however, several major exposures that have to do with the business itself.

Key Persons Losses

What would happen to your business if an accident or illness made it impossible for you to work? What if one of your partners or your sales manager were to die suddenly? Most of us would rather not think about such a "what if." Nevertheless, it is important for you to prepare your business for survival, long before a key person dies or is disabled. Unfortunately, it is a step that is often overlooked.

The following questions address a few problems that may occur.

How will the business survive if the owner becomes seriously ill or disabled?

What will the owner's source of income be? How will it be treated for tax purposes?

Who would "take over" so that the business can continue?

What if that person is not qualified or is a minor?

Suppose the owner dies?

If a will is not in place before the owner's death, what happens to the business? Does it close? Does someone inherit? Who?

If the owner's life savings have been invested in the business, will the surviving family have to watch those savings go down the drain because no one knows what to do or how to do it?

What will the surviving family's source of income be while the future of the business is being decided?

If the business is to be sold, where will working capital come from for the transition period?

How is the fair market value of the business to be determined?

Would the fair market value be apt to change because of the loss of a key person?

If the business forms the bulk of the estate, what are the tax implications for the surviving spouse and heirs?

Is there some pre-death strategy that could minimize that tax liability?

The answers to these questions can best be determined with the help of the professionals on your business's planning team: your attorney, accountant and insurance agent. Their expertise in estate planning, financial planning, current legal and tax codes will help you develop a plan for your business's survival and a way of implementing it.

Suppose the business is a partnership and one of the partners dies?

Unless the partners have prepared some other binding arrangement, that is already in place, their partnership is dissolved when one of them dies.

The duties of the surviving partner(s) are limited to winding up the affairs of the partnership.

The surviving partner(s) will be personally liable for losses that the business's assets are insufficient to cover.

The partners may have to set up agreements that provide for the surviving partner's purchase of a deceased partner's interest at a prearranged valuation. Business life insurance of each partner could provide the fund the survivors need to purchase the deceased partner's interest.

Who should pay the premium? The business? Each partner?

What are the pros and cons of these alternatives?

What are the tax implications of each?

How would each affect the firm's cash flow?

There are many plans and many ways to set them up. Your planning team can suggest a wide range of options compatible with your needs, your firm's cash position and tax implications.

What if the business is incorporated?

In most small incorporated businesses there are only a few stockholders, and most of them take an active part in running the business.

Death of a major stockholder often throws a spotlight on the survivors' differences. Conflict or major personality clashes can seriously threaten the survival of the firm. Dissension also damages employee morale, can lead to a loss of business and may even harm the firm's credit rating.

Unless otherwise provided for, the deceased major stockholder's shares will become part of his or her estate. While the estate is being settled, the estate administrator can vote (i.e., exercise the right to control) the stock. If a controlling interest in the firm is involved, he or she could name a new board of directors and take over full control of the corporation.

What if the heirs decide to get involved in the business? If they decide to retain the stock, will it provide enough income for them to live on?

If the heirs decide to sell, would they be required to offer the other major stockholders first refusal?

Could some plan be set up that would allow the surviving stockholders to finance a buy-out of the heirs' holdings?

Without such a plan, would the remaining stockholders' search for buy-out funds have any impact upon the firm's credit?

Once again, planning is essential. Your attorney, accountant and insurance agent can develop a legally binding strategy to prevent outsiders from unexpectedly coming into the business and to ensure an orderly "changing of the guard" should a major stockholder die.

The Key Person Exposure

Do not overlook what would happen if you were to suddenly lose the services of a key person (who is not an owner, partner or major stockholder) because of illness, disability or death (e.g., a sales manager or the office manager/bookkeeper).

What impact would that person's absence have on sales volume? Costs? Productivity? Efficiency? The firm's credit?

How would you reassign duties to cover the missing person's functions?

What extra costs would you have to incur to recruit a replacement?

How long would it take before the replacement is trained and productive?

The way you answer these questions depends on many factors, such as the kind of employee benefits already in place.

7. Loss Exposures and Risk Management

The next two steps of the risk management process are similar to those we face in managing our personal finances.

1. Loss control: What can be done to prevent or limit exposure to loss?

2. What techniques can be used to assure that funds will be available for losses that cannot be avoided or prevented?

Loss Control

Preventing or Limiting Exposure to Loss

One principle of loss prevention and control is the same in business as it is in your personal life: avoid activities that are too hazardous. For example: A merchant may decide not to sell a particular product because it is likely to injure customers; thereby, the firm avoids a product-liability exposure. For example: If you can't avoid an exposure completely, minimize it.

An apartment owner may decide against constructing a new building on a rural hillside site that has a long history of brush fires. Instead, he builds on suburban, level land, which is supplied by town water and is two minutes from a fire station. While exposure of loss from fire can seldom be eliminated completely, this owner has reduced the possible severity of loss by choosing a safer site closer to the fire-fighting services.

Look again to see if the extent of possible loss can be further reduced.

That same apartment owner, for example, may decide to build using fire-resistant construction and materials. thereby reducing the chance of fire spreading. He may also decide to install smoke detectors, fire alarms and automatic extinguishing systems throughout the building to further reduce the severity and spread of fire.

Risk Retention

A business owner may decide that the firm can afford to absorb some losses, either because the frequency and probability of loss are low or because the value of loss is manageable.

A firm owns several business vehicles. The drivers have an excellent safety record, and exposure to collision is low because these vans cover uncongested rural routes. Because these are older vehicles, their book value has decreased substantially.

Rather than continue to pay for collision insurance on the vans, the firm decides to drop the collision coverage completely. If an accident damages one or more of the vans, the firm will pay for collision damage with company funds. In effect, the firm has decided to retain the risk itself rather than transfer the risk to an insurance company by paying for collision insurance.

Or the firm could decide to retain part of the risk and insure the rest.

Transferring Risk

Another method of managing exposure to loss is by transferring the risk. Although most businesses do this by buying insurance (which transfers some or all of the risk to the insurance company), there are other non-insurance options.

The firm may decide to eliminate the collision exposure completely by selling the firm's vans and hiring a local delivery service. This solution eliminates not only the collision exposure, but also the exposures associated with owning and maintaining the vans. In effect, the firm has transferred all of the expenses to the local delivery service.

To reduce exposure to property damage, a retailer may decide to cut in-store inventories and to handle certain items only on a special-order basis. The owner will place small reorders with suppliers more frequently. The result? Lower inventory values in the store, therefore a lower exposure. The retailer is actually transferring much of the exposure of property loss to the suppliers.

Insurance as a Risk Strategy

The most common method of transferring risk is insurance. By insuring your home and your car, you have transferred much of the risk of loss to the company that issued the policy. You pay a relatively small amount in premium rather than run the risk of not protecting yourself against the possibility of a much larger financial loss.

In business insurance, as in personal insurance, only you can decide which exposures you absolutely must insure against. Some decisions, however, are already made for you:

those required by law (such as workers' compensation).

those that others require. For example, you cannot register or operate a business vehicle in most locations unless you can prove that it is insured. Similarly, few lenders will finance property acquisition or construction unless it is adequately insured, and unless they are named on the policy as having an insurable interest.

Today, very few businesses or individuals have sufficient cash or financial reserves to protect themselves against the hundreds of property and liability exposures that most businesses face.

What those exposures are, what their dollar value is and how much protection is enough, are thorny questions. When you add the need for an employee benefits program, the need to protect the business when its ownership or management changes, the picture becomes increasingly complex. That is why the experience and professional knowledge of an insurance agent are so important in helping you cover all the bases.

The Role of the Insurance Professional

The agent is the insurance industry's primary client representative. Typically, the independent agent is a small-business owner and manager. By using this distribution system, insurance companies are represented by agents who receive a commission for selling the companies' products and services. An agent may represent more than one insurance company.

The professional independent insurance agent has been trained in risk analysis. He or she is familiar with the insurance coverages and financial strategies available in your place, and with the regulations that govern them. With this expertise, the agent can point out exposures you may otherwise overlook.

Finally, your insurance professional can help you develop possible solutions. You make the final decisions, but your agent can suggest options from a vast menu of risk management strategies. He or she has the technical knowledge to amend a basic policy by adding special coverages and endorsements. The resulting policy will be custom-tailored to your business's unique protection needs.

Your agent can also recommend non-insurance

strategies to meet your needs. Where appropriate, he or she will suggest that your accountant and attorney be brought into the decision-making process to review the legal and tax implications of suggested strategies.

Other Services Insurers Provide

You may not be aware of some of the other services that insurance companies provide to policyholders.

Legal defense. Liability insurance coverages (particularly for property damage and bodily injury) usually include legal defense at no additional charge when the policy- holder is named a party to a lawsuit that involves a claim covered, by the policy. Litigation is costly, whether the claimant's suit is valid or ridiculous. The legal defense provision greatly reduces those costs.

Inspection services. Many cities require businesses to conduct regular inspections of the steam boilers in commercial buildings. Boiler and machinery insurance policies not only protect against certain kinds of damage to energy equipment but also provide for inspection by the insurance company's specialists. The insurance company issues a certificate of inspection to the policyholder as proof that the inspection requirement has been met.

Loss control services. Some commercial insurance policyholders may also qualify for consulting services of the insuring company's Loss Control (or Engineering) Department. This department is staffed with engineers and safety experts who specialize in inspecting business premises, identifying hazards, perils and possible trouble spots and in recommending possible solutions.

8. Insurance Checklist for Small Business

In addition to helping you identify, minimize and in some instances eliminate business risks, this checklist will help you strengthen your insurance program and provide guidelines for discussions you should have with a qualified insurance professional.

The points covered are grouped under three general headings: 1) coverages that are essential for most businesses; 2) coverages that are desirable for many firms; and 3) coverages for employee benefits.

This checklist is followed by a brief discussion of four basic steps that are necessary for good insurance management: 1) Recognize the risks to which you are exposed. 2) Follow the guides for buying insurance economically. 3) Have a plan. 4) Get professional advice.

Some small-business owners look on insurance as if it were a sort of tax. They recognize that it is necessary but consider it a burdensome expense that should be kept at a minimum. Is this view justified?

Not if you take a more conservative approach. You can use insurance to get many positive advantages, as well as the negative one of avoiding losses. Used correctly, insurance can contribute a great deal to your success by reducing the uncertainties under which you operate. It can reduce employee turnover, improve your credit at the bank, make it easier to sell customers on favorable terms and help keep your business going in case an insured peril interrupts operations. The potential benefits of good insurance management make it well worth your study and attention.

Checklist

The points covered in the checklist are grouped under three general classes of insurance: 1) coverages that are essential for most businesses, 2) coverages that are desirable for many firms but not absolutely necessary and 3) coverages for employee benefits. For each of the statements, put a check if you understand the statement and how it affects your insurance program. Then study your policies with these points in mind and discuss with your agent questions you still have.

Essential Coverages

Four kinds of insurance are essential: fire, liability, automobile, and workers' compensation insurance.

In some areas and in some kinds of business, crime insurance, which is discussed under "Desirable Coverage," is also essential.

Are you certain that all the following points have been given full consideration in your insurance program?

Fire Insurance

1. You can add other perils-such as windstorm, hail, smoke, explosion, vandalism and malicious mischief - to your basic fire insurance at a relatively small additional fee.

2. If you need comprehensive coverage, your best buy may be one of the all-risk contracts that offer the broadest available protection for the money.

3. The insurance company may indemnify you - that is, compensate you for your losses in any one of several ways: (1) It may pay actual cash value of the property at the time of loss. (2) It may repair or replace the property with material of like kind and quality. (3) It may take all the property at the agreed or appraised value and reimburse you for your loss.

4. You can insure property you don't own. You must have an insurable interest - a financial interest

- in the property when a loss occurs but not necessarily at the time the insurance contract is made. For instance, a repair shop or dry-cleaning plant may carry insurance on customers' property in the shop, or you may hold a mortgage on a building and insure the building although you don't own it.

5. When you sell property, you cannot assign the insurance policy along with the property unless you have permission from the insurance company.

6. Even if you have several policies on your property, you can still collect only the amount of your actual cash loss. All the insurers share the payment proportionately. Suppose, for example, that you are carrying two policies one for $20,000 and one for $30,000 - on a $40,000 building, and fire causes damage to the building amounting to $12,000. The $20,000 policy will pay $4,800, The $30,000 policy will pay $7,200;

7. Special protection other than the standard fire insurance policy is needed to cover the loss by fire of accounts, bills, currency, deeds, evidence of debt and money and securities.

8. If an insured building is vacant or unoccupied for more than 60 consecutive days, coverage is

suspended unless you have a special endorsement to your policy canceling this provision.

9. If, either before or after a loss, you conceal or misrepresent to the insurer any material fact or circumstance concerning your insurance or the interest of the insured, the policy may be voided.

10. If you increase the hazard of fire the insurance company may suspend your coverage even for losses not originating from the increased hazard. (An example of such a hazard might be renting part of your building to a cleaning plant.)

11. After a loss, you must use all reasonable means to protect the property from further loss or run the risk of having your coverage canceled.

12. To recover your loss, you must furnish within 60 days (unless an extension is granted by the insurance company) a complete inventory of the damaged, destroyed and undamaged property showing in detail quantities, costs, actual cash value and amount of loss claimed.

13. If you and the insurer disagree on the amount of loss, the question may be resolved through special appraisal procedures provided for in the fire-

insurance policy.

14 You may cancel your policy without notice at any time and get part of the premium returned. The insurance company also may cancel at any time with a 5-day written notice to you.

15. By accepting a coinsurance clause in your policy, you get a substantial reduction in premiums. A coinsurance clause states that you must carry insurance equal to 80 or 90 percent of the value of the insured property. If you carry less than this, you cannot collect the full amount of your loss, even if the loss is small. What percent of your loss you can collect will depend on what percent of the full value of the property you have insured it for.

16. If your loss is caused by someone else's negligence, the insurer has the right to sue this negligent third party for the amount it has paid you under the policy. This is known as the insurer's right of subrogation. However, the insurer will usually waive this right upon request. For example, if you have leased your insured building to someone and have waived your right to recover from the tenant for any insured damages to your property, you should have your agent request the insurer to waive

the subrogation clause in the fire policy on your leased building.

17. A building under construction can be insured for fire, lightning, extended coverage, vandalism and malicious mischief.

Liability

1. Legal liability limits of $1 million are not considered high or unreasonable even for a small business.

2. Most liability policies require you to notify the insurer immediately after an incident on your property that might cause a future claim. This holds true no matter how unimportant the incident may seem at the time it happens.

3. Most liability policies, in addition to bodily injuries, may now cover personal injuries (libel, slander and so on) if these are specifically insured.

4. Under certain conditions, your business may be subject to damage claims even from trespassers.

5. You may be legally liable for damages even in cases where you used "reasonable care."

6. Even if the suit against you is false or fraudulent,

the liability insurer pays court costs, legal fees and interest on judgments in addition to the liability judgments themselves.

7. You can be liable for the acts of others under contracts you have signed with them. This liability is insurable.

8. In some cases you may be held liable for fire loss to property of others in your care. Yet, this property would normally not be covered by your fire or general liability insurance. This risk can be covered by fire legal liability insurance or through requesting subrogation waivers from insurers of owners of the property.

Automobile Insurance

1. When an employee or a subcontractor uses a car on your behalf, you can be legally liable even though you don't own the car or truck.

2. Five or more automobiles or motorcycles under one ownership and operated as a fleet for business purposes can generally be insured under a low-cost fleet policy against both material damage to your vehicle and liability to others for property damage or personal injury.

3. You can often get deductibles of almost any amount and thereby reduce your premiums.

4. Automobile medical-payments insurance pays for medical claims, including your own, arising from automobile accidents regardless of the question of negligence.

5. In most States, you must carry liability insurance or be prepared to provide other proof (surety bond) of financial responsibility when you are involved in an accident.

6. Even if the suit against you is false or fraudulent, the liability insurer pays court costs, legal fees and interest on judgments in addition to the liability judgments themselves.

7. You can be liable for the acts of others under contracts you have signed with them. This liability is insurable.

8. In some cases you may be held liable for fire loss to property of others in your care. Yet, this property would normally not be covered by your fire or general liability insurance.

This risk can be covered by fire legal liability insurance or through requesting subrogation waivers from insurers of owners of the property.

Desirable Coverages

Some types of insurance coverage, while not absolutely essential, will add greatly to the security of your business. These coverages include business-interruption insurance, crime insurance, glass insurance and rent insurance.

Business Interruption Insurance

1. You can purchase insurance to cover fixed expenses that would continue if a fire shut down your business - such as salaries to key employees, taxes, interest. depreciation and utilities - as well as the profits you would lose.

2. Under properly written contingent business - interruption insurance, you can also collect if fire or other peril closes down the business of a supplier or customer and this interrupts your business.

3. The business - interruption policy provides payments for amounts you spend to hasten the reopening of your business after a fire or other insured peril.

4. You can get coverage for the extra expenses you

suffer if an insured peril while not actually closing your business down, seriously disrupts it.

5. When the policy is properly endorsed,

you can get business-interruption insurance to indemnify you if your operations are suspended because of failure or interruption of the supply of power, light, heat, gas or water furnished by a public utility company.

Crime Insurance

1. Burglary insurance excludes such property as accounts, fur articles in a showcase window and manuscripts.

2. Coverage is granted under burglary insurance only if there are visible marks of the burglar's forced entry.

3. Burglary insurance can be written to cover, in addition to money in a safe, inventoried merchandise and damage incurred in the course of a burglary.

4. Robbery insurance protects you from loss of property, money and securities by force, trickery or threat of violence on or off your premises.

5. A comprehensive crime policy written just for small business owners is available. In addition to burglary and robbery, it covers other types of loss by theft, destruction and disappearance of money and securities. It also covers thefts by your employees.

Glass Insurance

1. You can purchase a special glass insurance policy that covers all risk to plate-glass windows, glass signs, motion-picture screens, glass brick, glass doors, showcases, countertops and insulated glass panels.

2. The glass-insurance policy covers not only the glass itself, but also its lettering and ornamentation, if these are specifically insured, and the costs of temporary plates or boarding up when necessary.

3. After the glass has been replaced, full coverage is continued without any additional premium for the period covered.

Rent Insurance

1. You can buy rent insurance that will pay your rent if the property you lease becomes unusable because of fire or other insured perils and your lease

calls for continued payments in such a situation.

2. If you own property and lease it to others, you can insure against loss if the lease is canceled because of fire and you have to rent the property again at a reduced rental.

Employee Benefit Coverages

Insurance coverages that can be used to provide employee benefits include group life insurance, group health insurance, disability insurance and retirement income.

Key-man insurance protects the company against financial loss caused by the death of a valuable employee or partner.

Disability Insurance

1. Workers' compensation insurance pays an employee only for time lost because of work injuries and work-related sickness- not for time lost because of disabilities incurred off the job. But you can purchase, at a low premium, insurance to replace the lost income of workers who suffer short-term or long-term disability not related to work.

2. You can get coverage that provides employees with an income for life in case of permanent disability resulting from work related sickness or accident.

9. Organizing Your Insurance Program

A sound insurance protection plan is just as important to the success of your business as good financing, marketing, personnel management or any other business function. And like the other functions, good risk and insurance management is not achieved by accident, but by organization and planning.

A lifetime of work and dreams can be lost in a few minutes if your insurance program does not include certain elements.

To make sure that you are covered, you should take action in four distinct ways:

1. Recognize the various ways you can suffer loss.

2. Follow the guides for buying insurance economically.

3. Organize your insurance-management program.

4. Get professional advice.

Recognize the risks. The first step toward good protection is to recognize the risks you face and make up your mind to do something about them. Wishful thinking or an it-can't-happen-to-me attitude won't lessen or remove the possibility that a ruinous misfortune may strike your business.

Some businesses will need coverages not mentioned in the checklist. For example, if you use costly professional tools or equipment in your business, you may need special insurance covering loss or damage to the equipment or business interruption resulting from not being able to use the equipment.

Study insurance costs. Before you purchase insurance, investigate the methods by which you can reduce the costs of your coverage. Be sure to cover the following points:

1. Decide what perils to insure against and how much loss you might suffer from each.

2. Cover your largest loss exposure first.

3. Use as high a deductible as you can afford.

4. Avoid duplication in insurance.

5. Buy in as large a unit as possible. Many of the "package policies" are very suitable for the types of small businesses they are designed to serve, and often they are the only way a small business can get really adequate protection.

6. Review your insurance program periodically to make sure that your coverage is adequate and your premiums are as low as possible yet consistent with sound protection.

Have a plan. To manage your insurance program for good coverage at the lowest possible cost, you will need a definite plan that undergirds the objectives of your business. Here are some suggestions for good risk and insurance management:

1. Write down a clear statement of what you expect insurance to do for your firm.

2. Select only one agent to handle your insurance. Having more than one may spread and weaken responsibility.

3. If an employer or partner is going to be responsible for your insurance program, be sure he/she understands the responsibility.

4. Do everything possible to prevent losses and to keep those that do occur as low as possible.

5. Don't withhold from your insurance agent important information about your business and its exposure to loss. Treat your agent as a professional

helper.

6. Don't try to save money by underinsuring or by not covering some perils that could cause loss, even though you think the probability of their occurring is very small. If the probability of loss is really small, the premium will also be small.

7. Keep complete records of your insurance policies, premiums paid, losses and loss recoveries. This information will help you get better coverage at lower costs in the future.

8. Have your property appraised periodically by independent appraisers. This will keep you informed of what your exposures are, and you will be better able to prove what your actual losses are if any occur.

Get professional advice about your insurance. Insurance is a complex and detailed subject. A professionally qualified agent, broker or consultant can explain the options, recommend the right coverage and help you avoid financial loss.

10. Glossary of Insurance Terms

ADJUSTER. A person who settles insurance claims. An adjuster may be a Travelers employee or an independent operator.

ADJUSTMENT. The settlement of a claim; final premium determination.

AGENT'S AUTHORITY. The authority placed in the agent by the insurance company; the extent to which the agent may act on behalf of the company. This authority is defined by a contract between the agent and the company.

ALL-RISK. A term commonly used to describe broad forms of Property or Liability coverages. It is misleading because no Property or Liability Policy is truly an ALL-RISK coverage. A Policy will invariably contain some exclusions.

APPRAISAL. An estimate of value, loss or damage.

ASSIGNED RISK. A risk that has been declined by one or more companies. Such a risk may be assigned to designated companies by a recognized authority. The operation is called an Assigned Risk Plan.

ASSURED. The insured; the one for whom insurance is written.

BASIC BENEFITS. Basic benefits, generally, are all the benefits offered by a group health plan except major medical. Basic benefits may include hospital, surgical and medical expense insurance: supplemental accident, diagnostic lab and X-ray, radiation therapy and dental expense insurance.

BENEFICIARY. A person who will receive policy benefits.

BENEFIT FORMULA. A benefit formula defines the amounts of life insurance that may be purchased for employees in a specific classification (salary, occupation, length of service).

BENEFIT. That amount payable under an insurance policy because of an accident, injury or illness.

BINDER. An agreement, usually written, whereby one party agrees to insure another party pending receipt of a final action upon the application.

BUSINESS INTERRUPTION. Insurance covering the loss of earnings resulting from the destruction of property: called Use and Occupancy Insurance.

CANCELLATION. The terminating of an insurance contract by either the insurance company or the insured.

CARRIER. An insurance company.

CASH DEDUCTIBLE. The amount of money an insured must pay for covered expenses before certain benefits can begin.

CASH VALUE. The value, in cash, of a life insurance policy.

CASUALTY. An accident, occurrence or event; the person to whom it happens; the general insurance term applied to insurance coverages for an accident, occurrence or event.

CERTLET. A booklet that describes the benefits and all the provisions of a group policy that affect the insured. The certlet becomes a certification of insurance when the person is eligible for the insurance. It is then the legal document that proves the person is actually insured.

CLAIM. A request by an insured for benefits under an insurance policy.

COINSURANCE. Two or more entities providing

insurance protection and sharing in losses.

COMPENSATION. Wages, salaries, awards, fees, commissions; any return in payment for a financial loss.

COMPREHENSIVE. A loosely used term signifying broad or extensive insurance coverage.

CONTRIBUTORY. A group insurance plan that is paid partly by employees' contributions and partly by the employer's contributions.

CONTRIBUTORY NEGLIGENCE. Partial responsibility for one's own injury or damage.

COVERAGE. The insurance protection provided by the policy.

DECLARATIONS. That part of an insurance policy containing the information about the applicant that the applicant listed on the application for insurance.

DEDUCTIBLE. An amount the insured must pay before insurance benefits may be paid.

DISCOUNT. A reduction applied to an insurance premium because of good experience, for example.

DRAFT. A financial instrument similar to a check frequently used by insurance companies to pay losses.

EFFECTIVE DATE. The date the policy is put in force; the inception date.

ENDORSEMENT. A written amendment affecting the declarations, insuring agreements, exclusions or conditions of an insurance policy; a rider.

EVIDENCE OF INSURABILITY, Medical proof, from either a questionnaire or a physical examination, that an applicant, employee or dependent is healthy and, therefore, insurable.

EXAMINER. An individual who reviews, evaluates and processes claims.

EXCLUSION. That which is expressly eliminated from the coverage of an insurance policy.

EXPIRATION DATE. The date an insurance policy terminates.

EXPOSURE. Person or property, injury to whom or damage to which will cause an economic loss.

FACE AMOUNT. In life insurance, the amount of basic coverage stated on the face of the policy.

GRACE PERIOD. A period beyond the premium-due date, during which the premium may be paid and the insurance will be continued in force.

GROUP INSURANCE. Insurance covering a group of employees.

HAZARD. A condition that creates or increases the probability of a loss.

HEALTH INSURANCE. Commonly called Accident and health Insurance, protection against financial loss from a personal accident or illness.

INCURRED LOSS. A loss that, while not yet paid, has been sustained and for which reserves have been established to pay in the future.

INDEMNITY. Insurance protection that will place the insured in the same financial position as before a loss was sustained.

INSPECTION. An examination by those having authority. An insurance company usually reserves the right to inspect any property it insures.

INSURANCE. Protection against loss. The insured sacrifices a small certain loss (the premium) for protection against a large uncertain loss (an accident, fire, death). The insurance company assumes the risk by employing the law of large numbers and the principle of risk spreading.

INSURED. The entity whose life or property is protected by the insurance. The one for whom insurance is written.

LAPSE. To fail to continue an insurance policy; to cease to provide insurance protection.

LIABILITY. Being bound by law and justice to do something that may be enforced by the courts.

LIMITS. The value or amount of a policy; the greatest amount that can be collected under the policy.

LOSS. In insurance, the amount the insurer is required to pay because of an insurer's loss.

MULTI PERIL. An insurance policy that provides coverage against many perils. Sometimes called a "package" policy.

OCCURRENCE. A continuance of a repeated exposure to conditions which result in injury.

PERIL. Anything that may cause a loss (cause of a possible loss).

POLICY. A legal contract of insurance.

POLICYHOLDER. The owner of the policy; the one who purchases the policy and pays the premiums.

POLICY PERIOD. The term for which insurance remains in force, sometimes definite, sometimes not.

PREMIUM. The cost of an insurance policy. The charge the policyholder pays for the insurance protection.

PROPERTY. The thing owned; real property is real estate and things attached to it; anything else is personal property.

PROPERTY DAMAGE. Physical damage to property.

PROVISIONS. The terms or conditions of an insurance policy.

RATE. Cost per unit of insurance.

REINSTATE. To restore coverage after it has been canceled or suspended.

REINSURANCE. Insurance placed by an

underwriter in another company to reduce the amount of the risk his or her company has assumed.

RENEW. To continue; to replace as with a new policy.

RIDER. An endorsement.

SCHEDULE OF BENEFITS. The amount of insurance for which each classification of employees is eligible. (Classifications can be based on salary, wage, occupation or length of service.)

SELF-INSURANCE. An arrangement where, instead of purchasing an insurance policy, a party maintains a reserve fund to protect it against a loss.

SETTLEMENT OPTION. The way in which money for the death benefit of an insurance policy will be paid to a beneficiary.

SURETY. A guarantee that a person, normally called the principal, will perform according to a statute or a contract. Surety offers protection to a third party, normally called an obligee.

UNDERWRITER. The insurance company; a party assuming the risk; the person performing the underwriting function.

VOID. Of no force; null.

WAITING PERIOD. A period immediately after the inception of the policy, during which no benefits will be paid even if a loss occurs. Pertains to health insurance.

WAIVER OF PREMIUM. In life insurance, a provision which states that, if the insured becomes disabled and the disability appears total and permanent, the insurance policy will continue in full force without further payment or premium.